D1709308

Library of Congress Catalog Number: TXU 1-585-683
ISBN Number: ISBN: 978-0-615-25259-9

Very early in the morning, Buddy, the big city bus wakes up in his bus garage. He opens his eyes wide, starts his motor and heads off to work.

His first passenger of the day is Mr. Leffer who is going to work.
"Good morning Mr. Leffer, how are you?"
"Hello, Buddy, you're right on time."

They ride past the fire station and down toward the Market. Mrs. Sherman is waiting there and waves for Buddy to stop. "Hi Mrs. Sherman, come on in, said Buddy." "Oh thank you Buddy, it's good to see you."

Buddy is happy to have some passengers. He heads over the bridge and winds around the park. Birds are singing a very cheerful song this morning. It makes Buddy smile.

At the next corner, Mrs. Williams and her daughter Betty are waiting. Betty jumps up and down and points when she sees Buddy coming.

A couple blocks later, Mr. Leffer, rings the bell. This tells Buddy his stop is coming up. "Have a good day at work Mr. Leffer," Buddy says. "Ok, Buddy, I'll see you again soon."

Buddy, turns down Leafy Lane and drives through a long, dark tunnel. This was Betty's favorite part of the trip. She smiled at her mom and held on tight.

The bell rang again. Mrs. Sherman's house was just ahead. Buddy slowed down and stopped. He opened the back doors for Mrs. Sherman. "Thank you, Buddy, I enjoyed the ride." "You're welcome Mrs. Sherman. Have a good day."

"That just leaves us," Buddy said to Mrs. Williams and Betty. "We have you all to ourselves," Betty said. Buddy liked that. He liked all his passengers and enjoyed their company very much.

"The doctor's office is just on the next block Buddy, so we'll have to leave you soon," said Mrs. Williams. Buddy saw the sign on the big brick building "Dr. Shapiro." "I see it said Buddy."

He stopped and let Mrs. Williams and Betty off. "Thanks Buddy, see you later," said Betty. "Good-bye, Buddy," said Mrs. Williams. "Good-bye said Buddy. Good luck with your check up... and your knee!

Buddy pulled away and started down Main Street again. But he started to feel sad. His bus was empty. All of his friends had gotten off and gone on their way. Now he was alone.

Maybe someone will be waiting
at the next bus stop he thought.
But no. No one was there.

Maybe by the train station. No one there, either. Buddy got to the end of the line and turned around. Still no passengers. He started back down Main Street, feeling sad and lonely.

But just then, he saw someone. "Could it be?" Buddy said to himself? "IT IS!" "Someone is waiting for a ride!" "He's waiting for ME."

"Hello, my name is Buddy. Do you need a ride?" "Yes, yes I do," said the man. "I'm going to my grand daughter's house. She lives on the other side of town. It's her birthday." "Your granddaughter's birthday? How wonderful," said Buddy. "I'll be glad to take you there."

"Yes," She lives on Sunny Street."
"I know right where that is,
"Buddy said.
"You're very helpful, Buddy. You
tell me when I need to get off."

Just then, Buddy saw two girls waving at him. "They were just getting out of school. It was about that time in the afternoon now. "Stop! Stop! They shouted." "Hi girls, are you headed home from school?" Buddy asked.

"No, we're going to the park," they said. "I know the one," said Buddy. "We'll be there in a jiffy."

At the very next stop, two boys, one tall and one small, were waiting under the bus stop with handfuls of books. "Hi there young fellas, where are you going with all those books?" "We have to return them to the library and we have to get there before they close." "I won't let you down," said Buddy. "Hop in."

The library was the very next stop on Buddy's route. Buddy pulled up right in front and the boys jumped through the front doors and ran as fast as they could. "Bye, thank you for the ride," they shouted over their shoulders.

Buddy turned left down Breezy Lane to the park. "Here you go, girls," he said. And your stop is coming up next, sir" Buddy told the man with the present. "Thanks, Buddy, I'm ready," the man said.

"Here we are, sir" Buddy said.
"Thank you, Buddy. It was a very nice ride.
I hope I see you again."
"Me, too," Buddy said with a smile. Have fun at the birthday party!

Now Buddy was just a few blocks from the garage where he started his day. It was time for him to turn in for the night. As he pulled into the garage, he started to feel sad again. His day was done. There was no one else to pick up. No more rides to give.

But, just then he remembered something... and he got a big smile on his face. He knew that in the morning, he would get to do it all over again. That made him very happy.

Buddy closed his eyes and dreamt about how much fun he was going to have tomorrow. "That's what I like best about my job," Buddy thought, "there's always tomorrow."

The End

Made in the USA
Charleston, SC
19 October 2012